The Gift of Inner Peace
*Cycles and Seasons,
Symbols and Reasons*

by
Susan J. Ackerman

The Gift of Inner Peace

Copyright © 2019 by Susan J. Ackerman

All rights reserved

Photographs by Susan J. Ackerman

Printed in the United States

First Printing

1 2 3 4 5 6 7 8 9 10

ISBN 9781936711598

Railroad Street Press
394 Railroad St., Ste 2
St. Johnsbury, VT 05819

PREFACE

I wrote these pieces, one a month, over a period of years. What motivated me to write them? Having come through a difficult period in my own life in which I lost my entire family in one year, I was determined to regain the peace and joy I had previously known. Taking photographs for each chapter has helped me understand how Nature's messages can guide us to find Inner Peace. It has been a joyful process. I hope you, the reader, will find my discoveries helpful in your own search for Inner Peace.

I've divided the book into three sections: 1. *Cycles in the Seasons* illustrates how monthly messages from Nature support our practice of seeking peace. 2. *Symbols in the Months* shows us how to recognize hidden symbols in Nature. 3. Be*Cause and Effect* helps us understand that everything is a lesson. The more we understand and accept our lessons, the more peace we will have. This book offers keys to achieving lasting patience and Inner Peace. Of course, we are all a work in progress, but once peace becomes our priority, we can become better and better at creating it every day.

ACKNOWLEDGEMENTS

I want to thank Sandra Burkett, Marion Dunham, Barbara Baker, and Donna Crane for their excellent help with careful proofreading, wonderful clarifying suggestions and caring support.

My deep appreciation also goes to all my Guides and Angels for their constant support, love and inspiration.

Quotations in this book are from *The White Horse,* 1983 and *The Peaceful Climb,* 2007 by Yvonne Youst, Holly Publishing Company.

DEDICATION

I dedicate this book to all of us
who are searching
for greater Inner Peace.

Table of Contents

Preface, Acknowledgments, Dedication

Cycles in the Seasons	1
January, Seeing the Larger Picture	3
February, From Ego to Self	5
March, Flowing with Time	7
April, Reach Up	9
May, Making the Earth More Peaceful	11
June, Find the Positive in Change	13
July, The Power of Ripples	15
August, Reflections of Ourselves	17
September, Life is Change	19
October, Creating Harmony	21
November, Testing Our Faith	23
December, Joining Together	25
Symbols in the Months	27
January, Resolutions for Growth	29
February, Love Creates Peace	31
March, Sensing Change	33
April, Sending Out Our Light	35

May, Inner Blossoms	37
June, Water Your Self	40
July, Peaceful Patterns	42
August, The Gift of Who We Are	44
September, Seeing the Good	47
October, Your Beauty	49
November, Gratefulness is Peace	51
December, An Age of Change	53

BeCause and Effect	57
January, Acceptance	59
February, Symbols of Hope	61
March, Patience Creates Peace	63
April, Delightful Reactions	65
May, Feel the Hope	67
June, Clear Sight	69
July, Finding Home	72
August, The Gift of Balance	74
September, Becoming Better	76
October, Awareness Creates Peace	78
November, Deepening Our Peace	81
December, White, Light, and Snow	83
Epilogue	85
About the Author	87

Cycles in the Seasons

JANUARY -
Seeing the Larger Picture

Happy New Beginnings! The New Year has arrived, with or without the expected snowfall. No matter what happens in the world, the seasons will continue their cycles and we will continue to reach for more of our loving Divine Self every day.

The ancient custom of creating New Year's Resolutions is a symbol of our desire to improve, to do something better. It is a reflection of our ongoing growth.

As we look at the leafless branches now, we are reminded of our own need for clarity and simplicity. January asks us to look at the larger picture and not get bogged down by details. Winter itself outlines our need for peace in simple, clear colors. Even the blue in the sky reminds us we are like the ocean, many drops forming one entity. Unity is a major key in our search for peace. Thinking about how we are all alike helps us understand our common goal of reaching up for more peace. Yes, there are stragglers who don't seem to be headed toward peace. But in time, when they are ready, they will seek it too. When people know we are one, they will not harm one another.

When you look at the pond in this photo, you can feel its clarity and simplicity. You can see the unity in all its parts, creating one picture. It is, in fact, a picture of Winter's peace, joy and beauty. You may want to consider these thoughts:

- In spite of the stress, where do we find the greatest joy in our life?
- Where can we simplify our life?
- What can we do to increase our sense of unity?

The great Masters all reminded us we are here to love. The more we improve how we love the earth, its creatures and one another, the happier and more peace-filled we will be. That concept creates an eternal unity of growth as we constantly improve how we express our loving Selves.

I wish each and all of you a
Peace-filled, Joyful, Hopeful year!!

February - From Ego to Self

What an emotional time we live in. The currents of feeling run high on all sides. Turbulent emotions are the opposite of Inner Peace. As the tide of peace comes in, we wonder how we can be loving and kind to people who are angry, hateful, and unkind?

The answer lies in understanding the Ego and the Self. First, we must know that all of us have Ego and Self in differing amounts.

Our Self is our Divine Self. The Self is understanding, kind and loving. Our Self knows we are a work in progress and that we are always growing and learning. Our Ego, on the other hand, is the fearful part of us. The Ego is like a frightened child whose behavior ranges from being insecure, condescending, mad, sad, or impatient. Our Ego is accusing, blaming, judgmental, manipulative, and all the negative behaviors we dislike. Our Self knows that every person is different and tries to understand all sides of a question. The Self is compassionate and forgiving. Our Self evaluates another to understand them. It never judges anyone since it knows we are all here to learn and grow. The Ego is sure it's always right and that the other person is always wrong. Because of the Ego's fear of change, it wants to control everyone and everything. Our Ego never forgets an injury and never forgives.

Our Self has faith in positive outcomes. It sees the larger truth of life. It is calm, confident, peace-filled and optimistic. The Self knows we are here to become kinder, more loving and to deepen our faith in life. Our Ego has no faith in change or in positive outcomes, which is why it is always afraid the worst will happen.

Understanding the Ego helps us to love people who are acting in negative ways. We don't have to love the Ego but we have to understand its fear. Then, we can wait patiently and, like a loving parent, we can practice knowing that every Ego will find its way to becoming a Loving Self.

The journey from Ego to Self is from fear to faith. It is a path we are all walking on, side by side. The more we can observe the Ego in ourselves, the more understanding we can be of the Ego in others. Knowing we are all imperfect gives us greater compassion and helps us accept and love others unconditionally.

The more we live in our Self, the more Inner Peace we will have. Every change we make toward Self helps move the world toward Peace.

May we enjoy our growth and look forward to our changes.

MARCH - Flowing with Time

The fascinating month of March has arrived. It has so much to do. It has to create the movement toward Spring. What changes are we being asked to encompass in this active month?

First, we have to reconstruct our notion of time by having to move it forward an hour. That inspires questions about the nature of Time itself. I've noticed that if I feel like I have a lot of time to do something, I find I have all the time I need. But if I feel rushed, suddenly the clock seems to move forward so quickly that I am always behind. So, the question becomes ... Who is controlling Time? Certainly, my own mind has a major influence on its movement. What does it mean that we can decide to move it forward or backward at will? Is it really 5 am or is it another time? It has been said that when we leave this Earth to begin our next life, we come to see, at the appropriate moment, that time is both linear and circular. The present, past and future are actually one eternal circle. This allows souls, when they are ready and if they choose, to leave one century and return to a past, present or future century. Why? To give us infinite opportunities to grow, learn, improve, and love. This knowledge gives us much to ponder about Life's eternal cycle.

How can this knowledge affect our lives now? Since the Earth is a giant schoolroom where we are learning our chosen lessons, it evokes questions of: How much of your mental time do you spend thinking or fretting over the past? How much of your mental time do you spend planning for or fretting over the future? How much do you choose to live in the present? Since the past is over and the future is unknown, the only time we can truly affect is the present. And that's where all peace and happiness exist.

In March, we are being asked to flow, like the river in the photo, to wherever our mind and intuition take us and to adjust to any and all changes. The ability to go with the flow of time and life is a great gift and one worth focusing on and practicing, in the present moment, of course!

Spring is the beginning of new activity, even if winter teases us with a snowstorm or two. As we prepare to go out into the world of action, we will be less stressed if we emulate the river of Spring. If there are rocks and obstacles in our way, Spring reminds us to flow around them as we progress, knowing always that it will all be for the best. If someone in our lives can't yet understand this truth, all we can do is trust they will get there in their own timing. Like the river, we can be an inspiring example of faith in life's positive nature.

Happy Flowing!

APRIL –
Reach Up

"Spring is late this year.", the radio broadcaster announced this morning. That led me to thoughts about time and what is lateness. We call it late because we expect its manifestations to arrive sooner, as it has in previous years. Our expectations aren't allowing us to enjoy just exactly what spring is this year. But if we breathe in the air on a warm day, it smells just like spring air. If we open our senses to the feel of spring, it's right on schedule. In fact, everyone and everything is right on schedule...their own schedule. Were you called a Late Bloomer? Late by whose standards? Certainly not yours. You are right on track for what you wanted to be doing at this moment in your life.

This morning I heard the birds singing their spring song. I found myself thinking, "They know it's spring. They can smell it and feel it." That's where we humans often have difficulty. We don't trust what we feel. How many people only trust what they can see. Our Divine brain leads us to Truth all the time but it is our job to trust what we sense. That is part of our ongoing practice of peace. What does the month of April tell us? Perhaps its message is

Awake
Peace
Reach
Investigate
Life

The tiny shoots are awakening, reminding us that new life returns after a long winter's sleep. We are being asked now to reach for new heights of peace within ourselves, to awaken dreams we've had and investigate new ways of bringing them to fruition. Life beckons each of us to be our exciting, aware Self as we continue to grow and change with each new day. Let's climb the ladder of spiritual evolution together into this wonderful new time of opportunity.

Happy Growing!

MAY –
Making the Earth More Peaceful

May has arrived! It is our proof every year that no matter how long winter lasts, there will always be another spring. Growth is forever and the month of May is an ongoing demonstration of that truth.

In May, Nature draws our attention to the changes we see all around us. We need to remember that we are the guardians of the Earth, our beautiful, sacred home. Whenever we spend time outdoors, we are filled with a sense of peace. That is life's gift to us, given through Nature. May reminds us that we may return that gift and in gratitude, give our love to the Earth and all its creatures by making sure they are well and safe.

In contrast to the rapid pace of the world nowadays, May teaches us that real growth is slow but steady. I have learned that the slower I move, the more I can clearly observe and enjoy each amazing moment of life. That is one of May's great gifts to us all.

May is the moment when we till the soil of the past and plant our seeds for the future. The more thoughtful our seeds are, the sweeter their harvest will be. Here are some things you May want to consider.

• What seeds will you plant in your life this spring?

• What new ingredient will you put in the soil of today to fertilize the fruits of tomorrow?

• Have you chosen what will grow and what you wish to weed out?

• Where will you spread your love?

• What have you given yourself permission to do that will make the Earth a better place?

Perhaps the word "May" is a prayer for all we wish to come true. May we each receive the peace of Nature and find our own unique way to spread its gifts to everyone in our lives.

This spring, May we feel
an even deeper sense of wonder
from the beauty of our special home, the Earth.

JUNE –
Find the Positive in Change

All of a sudden, it's June. Despite the long winter, June has returned. I have heard so many people speak of the long winter we have just come through, promising they won't complain about the heat in the summer.

Even if this winter was colder than many, we are in a time of global warming and must remember the Earth is changing. Do we have the right to complain? Yes, of course. But what happens when we do? Instead of releasing the tension, we often prolong the pain. Summer will be hot and sometimes quite humid. Most of the people I know have difficulty with humidity; it makes us feel uncomfortable in our skin. But it is a part of life. Winters will probably get colder. Summers will probably be hotter with more humidity. Life is Change after all.

What can we do to practice maintaining our Inner Peace? Accept Change. Adapt to Change. Find something positive in Change and move forward knowing it is and will be a good thing. No one said that is easy, but it does work. It is up to each of us to continually find something positive in each thing that happens. When we do so, we have improved our understanding of life. And that is exciting.

This month's photo speaks of the beauty of summer, when all things that have been waiting as buds, reveal their gifts to us as blooms.   How will you share your blossoms with others this June?

The blossoming of lilacs and roses reminds us of the Peaceful Kingdom that was our home before we came to Earth. The beauty of all growing things fills us with the peace we all once knew. It asks us: How can we re-create that harmony, beauty and peace here on Earth? When we love ourselves, others and all of Nature, we are succeeding in what we came here to do. When we accept the change that is life and adapt happily to it, we live in and with peace.

Happy Searching!

JULY – The Power of Ripples

I stood at the edge of the lake and took this picture. The moment I entered the water, it changed from its placid, stationary state to all the ripples you see here. The ripples continued on and on and on to the far-reaching shore. I thought about what this might mean to each of us.

Many years ago, a dear friend taught me that everything we feel and think is felt by everyone we come into contact with. If we are feeling peaceful, it is received. If we are angry, it is felt. If we like someone, they feel it immediately. And if we don't, they feel that too. At first, I was surprised by this knowledge, thinking that if I wasn't liking someone but was pleasant with them, that it would be fine.

Once I understood that everyone feels everything we feel, even if they can't verbalize it, that changed everything. I chose to become aware of and be responsible for every thought and action. That caused a major shift in my life. That understanding guides my daily practice.

As you look at the scene, ask yourself what thoughts and feelings are you sending out? Are you aware of what they are? Are they peace-filled, loving thoughts?

Scientists tell us that water makes up 85% of our brain and 70% of the rest of our body. Like the lake, all our feelings ripple out from each of us and travel much farther than we know.

Because we want to create a caring world of peace, we have to be responsible for our thoughts and feelings. Peace begins one person at a time and ripples out from there.

Step into the lake of your life and consider the ripples you are creating.

AUGUST –
Reflections of Ourselves

The luxurious month of August has arrived. It's a time to breathe in and be even more aware of our blessings. Let's look at the word "August". Perhaps it stands for:

**Awareness.　Understanding.　Gratitude.
Unique Silent Thoughts.**

Heat asks us to move more slowly and look around at all our blessings. If we slow down and breathe in and out, we can become aware of the little things we may have taken for granted. We begin to notice the subtle reflections that are always there. Notice how the sunlight reflects on your car, on a wall, on you as you walk. Light is all around us but we tend to take it for granted. What is Light? It is a symbol for the presence of the Divine in each of us.

The longer you look, the more you begin to see how light creates reflections everywhere. In the photo, notice the reflection of the clouds in the stillness of the lake.

The people in our lives are like those clouds. They reflect back to us parts of ourselves. What do you see in the people around you? Are they reflecting your beauty, your kindness, your loving nature? And what about the people that annoy us or drive us crazy ... what are they reflecting? They are our lessons, parts of ourselves that we are in the process of improving. At first, we might say, "Oh no, I'm nothing like that." But if that were true, why do those people bother us so much unless it is a quiet unresolved part in us? As we work on the lessons these people teach us, it helps us to be more patient with them once we realize they are older parts of ourselves.

Patience becomes easier when we understand that we have all time to get better and better and better. There is no rush. And that brings us back to summer and the lesson of August. The more we take time to just enjoy the present moment and all of its wondrous Light, the more the gift of Inner Peace will soothe all the ripples on our surface.

I wish you a pleasing reflection
that will light up
your beautiful Self!

SEPTEMBER - Life is Change

The summer is ending and fall is beginning. I can hear faint groans of disappointment in the distance. To balance that reaction, we also know that whenever something ends something else begins.

We know it's a new time but what if we don't know what it has in store for us? How often do we have questions and have no answers? How do we maintain an inner sense of peace when our answer is "I don't know"? Not knowing the answer is a major test of our faith in Life and its positive outcomes. We can't know what's ahead of us, but we can believe that something good will come from it.

Recently my charming old wall clock stopped working. As I took it down and knew it couldn't be repaired, I knew I needed to purchase a new one. The new clock I bought is larger and less charming than the one I had. It has no scene in the background, only clear easy-to-read numbers. Then it dawned on me that this change was the symbol of a new time in my life. I still don't quite know what it means except I know that, like my new clock, I am to keep things simple and clear. Now, like all of us, I must wait patiently and with faith in the Positive for the information to be revealed.

    We know that every sunrise heralds a new day, a new beginning. The more carefully we look, the more we notice that there is something different about each day. Even though the months and seasons repeat themselves in an endless cycle, each day, each month, and each season has something unique. We have certainly observed that with the change in temperatures and weather everywhere. The question remains, What is new and different in this day, this month, and inside ourselves? If our reactions to situations or people are different than they were, that too, is a sign of a new time. When situations or people are upsetting, can we hold onto a sense of calm that helps us maintain our Inner Peace?

    We know that Change is the only constant in Life. It is our reaction to Change that defines our Inner Peace. The practice of believing there is something positive in all that's happening is our ongoing path to Inner Peace.

    This poem written by the late Yvonne Youst reminds us of our ongoing choice. It is one of my mantras.

> Each dawn will show two roads to take.
> The joyful one's a choice we make.

Happy peace-filled days!

OCTOBER - Creating Harmony

Welcome to the glory of October! Every October is different and yet they are also the same. Some years the colors are turning more slowly and we wonder if they will still be glorious. And then on a certain day, as if conducted by an unseen Conductor, the choir of colors arises and fills our eyes with wonder. Life keeps its promise to surround us with its autumnal beauty every year. And whether we doubt it or have faith that it will come, it appears to reassure and amaze us.

Every season brings us many messages. This October I would like to focus on its message of balance. The October photo echoes this message. We see many shades of each color, each one complementing the other. If we look at any one of them by itself, it does not stand out and yet, when taken together, they create a glorious scene.

They are a reminder that we need the harmony of balance in our lives. If we are talking a lot, we need the balance of silence. If we are very active, we need to balance it with stillness. If we are working too much, we need the balance of rest.

We can see this too, in life's contrasts. It is the dark of night that helps us appreciate the light of day. It is the cold of winter that helps us open to the warmth of spring. It is our difficulties that help us see how strong we've become. We can see our Self's strength more clearly when we compare it to our Ego's weakness. Every magnificent piece of art uses contrast to create its glorious message. Fall, in its many stages and colors, is like a choir that touches us with its harmonies.

This is a good moment to think about how you are harmonizing the many themes in your life. When I hear people say they are having difficulty with physical balance, I know they are needing to re-balance their lives since the body is a mirror of the soul. Have you woven your days and nights into a well-balanced masterpiece? If you haven't, what would you need to do to change that? If your life were a quilt, what changes would you make for it to be more satisfying and fulfilling?

If we look to Autumn's glory for answers, we can see that an appropriate balance is different for each person. As we search to improve our own, we can always look for the abundant messages all around us and we can ask for Guidance, trusting that it will always come at the perfect time. The balance of asking and following what we receive is another major key in our constant search for greater Inner Peace.

Happy seeking the symbols of Fall.

NOVEMBER – Testing Our Faith

November has returned, with its mysterious, haunting nature. As you look at this photo, you can almost feel it beckoning to you. It draws me into a story as yet unknown. I see it in the clouds, in the grasses, in the water. There is something in the character of this month that asks us to look back at memories and look forward with questions.

As we look ahead, we are reminded there is so much we cannot know. I often wake up in the morning and say to myself, "I know nothing and that's okay!" And then I laugh at all the questions whose answers I don't yet have.

November asks us to trust that we will have our answers at exactly the perfect moment whenever that is, knowing that is a part of faith. I define faith as believing that all will turn out for the good and that there is a Higher Power guiding us all along the way.

November is clearly a month that tests our faith. We don't see many sunshiny days or bright leaves on the trees. We can look back and remember the glorious autumn colors but they have gone for the moment. We have to look more deeply to see its haunting beauty. But the beauty is there, as it is in every season and every day.

We all have periods in our lives that seem more difficult, when we wonder how soon will it ease up. One important message of November is that Life is Change. Even the difficulties won't last forever. Every stage is replaced by a new one. We are all here to learn. Can we find something we can feel grateful for even in challenging times? Can we find our inner sunshine when the sun is not shining? Can we shine our sun for those who can't find it right now? As we answer "Yes" to these questions, our life becomes filled with greater joy and with greater Inner Peace.

Happy seeking and finding the gifts of Faith.

DECEMBER – Joining Together

I took this photo during a recent snowstorm. All the trees seemed to huddle together as they lasted out the storm. It made me think of the stormy times we live in and what a comfort it would be to gather together while waiting for the difficulties to pass.

Nature is such a wonderful teacher. The trees are unified just by being who they are. They don't think of their differences, but live side by side sharing sunrises and sunsets. Their roots are intertwined, reminding us of how connected we are.

In this magical month of December, I hope we will let Nature show us the way. The artistic dance of snowflakes as they search for a place to land holds a major key to joy. When I watch them, they seem to hold the essence of peace as they float through the air. They remind us that we are simultaneously, both separate and united. Once the flakes reach the Earth, we can no longer tell them apart. We just call them snow. I see snow as an inland ocean, teaching us that we have an Individual Self and a Universal Self that is part of all people. When I look at a field covered in magical white, I feel a sense of awe and Inner Peace. Why is that? It reminds me of how truly connected we all are.

One of the greatest gifts of December is reconnecting us to the deep peace we all hold inside ourselves, even if at times we forget that truth. Every time we help one another or help the Earth, like the trees in the photo, we join together. In those moments, we are re-creating the peace we all knew before we came to Earth. The inner knowledge of that peace is the greatest gift we have. It holds within it all Hope, all Love, and all Time.

My prayer is that all the people in our world will live in that peace in our lifetime.

I wish you all great Peace and Joy.

Symbols in the Months

JANUARY - Resolutions for Growth

January is an exciting time of year .... a brand new Beginning! Imagine we are sitting at the window looking out at the time yet to come. We can't see very far ahead of us but we can see all that is directly in front of us. If you look carefully, you will see on the left side of the photo, traces of a path we've walked, now freshly covered by a new snowfall. Memory, like that partially covered path, seems like a mirage reshaped by the lens of time and imagination. As we look at it, let's hold on to the best of what we've done. Then, let's remind ourselves that we'll make new tracks tomorrow.

When we look at this winter scene, we can feel a warm sense of camaraderie in the shapes created by the artistically placed stones. Looking at the three sculptures makes me realize how much our supportive friendships with one another strengthen our daily inner peace.

Allow yourself to be drawn into the peace of the photo and consider these resolutions.

- Look for the good in each day, no matter what is showing on the surface.
- Make some quiet time, even once a week, to send out your hopes and prayers for peace in the world.
- Think of your thoughts as seeds that prepare you for the hope of an abundant spring.
- Be grateful for winter days that give us time to rest and replenish ourselves.
- Resolve to do better in this New Year.

If we can learn to rejoice in every new beginning, knowing that Life is a good process, we will reap joy and happiness beyond what we have imagined as Life sends its abundant gifts to us.

If new beginnings make us uneasy, our practice is clear. We must strengthen our belief that all will be better in Time and choose to feel optimistic about every new start.

May we each add the Light of our optimism
to the purity and love we see
in the white of winter's true heart.

February - Love Creates Peace

As I thought about February, the message of Love seemed to call out to me. Down through the ages, many have tried to explain and describe love and it has always seemed to defy words.

What is Love? I think it is when we feel a complete acceptance and deep appreciation of all of Life, people, animals, and all of Nature. That's when we feel the greatest joy and peace.

It's easy to love those we already love but how can we love someone whose behavior is unacceptable? The simple answer comes from knowing the overview: Everyone has a frightened, mad or sad inner child called Ego and a joyful, loving Self. We can feel compassion for their Ego and love for their Self. We can know that everyone is on the same journey from fear to love and hope. This knowledge helps us accept where they are and not try to push them to move faster in their growth than they are ready for.

That is why it's so important to be in touch with our heart-mind. This is the part of us that feels the truth and sends its wisdom to the mind. The heart-mind is patient and forgiving. It understands that Life is an eternal journey toward greater Good. The heart sends its belief in the positive nature of Life to the mind. The heart's wisdom knows kindness, compassion, gratitude, joy and love, and sends its understanding to the mind. When we live in our heart-mind, we can understand the Ego and see the Self in every person.

Our Self knows that in time, we will all fully be the loving person we truly are inside. It understands that the Ego often expresses its fear in unloving ways. Remember that who we are is much more than what is showing.

Our Self is a piece of the Divine in each of us. It understands we are here to learn and grow, to understand and to love unconditionally. As we grow, we all continue to change our Ego into Self. Each time this happens, a spontaneous feeling of love and joy pours out from us. In those moments, we know that life is for love. Love is a healing power.

Love knows how to give and receive. As we look at all the signs of love around us, we become aware of how loved we are. The photo I took this month is a heart in a tree stump, reminding us we are loved.

Feeling love for all of Life creates unending Inner Peace. Love knows we are forever loved and loving.

Happy Month of Love!!!

MARCH - Sensing Change

    March, that elusive first month of spring. "Spring!" you say, "but there's nothing to let us know that it's spring with all that snow and ice. Who knows, we might get more snow tomorrow."

    March lures us with promises of warmer weather and tests us to see if we can know how it is different from February. The birds are singing a different song. They know the days are longer. And we do too. There is a different quality to the colder weather now. Like the birds, even the Earth knows the cold won't last.

    This is the exact moment when we are asked, not only to see what our eyes are seeing, but to sense the Change with our feelings. No two days are exactly alike. No two months are exactly alike. We are being asked to notice the difference and know that no matter how long winter seems to last, we are in Transition. In fact, the Change has already begun. Faith is our ability to know that Change is the only constant in Life. In Time, all Change will be for the Good. **M**arch, like every month, is a **m**arvelous teacher of that Truth.

When you hear people complaining about the cold and snow in March, you are listening to voices that are missing the overview. They do not understand that Life is constant Change. Think of times in your own life when you have been in Transition. You didn't quite know how to move ahead and yet you had to, not knowing what was ahead. How often did you find yourself saying, "But I don't have the answers I need."? Your question is the Answer. We have to learn to become comfortable with not knowing. We have to keep putting one foot in front of the other, trusting that we will know at the Perfect Time. It is more important to feel peace when you don't know. That is a sign you have made inner progress on the path of Peace.

Use the good detective inside your Self and search for what's different now. The more clearly we can see the path in front of us, the easier it is to move forward. Here are some helpful questions to consider. ✶ What signs let you know spring is coming? ✶ Can you feel spring arriving inside your Self? ✶ How have you changed from this time last spring? ✶ How well are you holding on to the Truth of Optimism, in spite of no visual evidence that things will improve?

Our Optimism is a major key to Inner Peace.

APRIL - Sending Out Our Light

    A new April has returned, different from the last one and yet, spring all the same. We are in-between the past of winter and the transition into a new spring. I think seasons exist to show us the cycles of life and to help us know there will always be another spring, another summer, fall and winter. Like waves on the ocean, they go out and return with new treasures in their currents. The ocean and the seasons are a constant reminder that life keeps changing but that every season has new gifts to bring us.
    The world itself is in a new season, a new Age, the Aquarian Age of major change. We are both the observers of this change but also the creators. If we focus every day on what is good about each moment and each day, we will find innumerable treasures that the day has brought us.

If we concentrate on peace in ourselves and peace in the world every day, our minds will send out that thought and create its reality in time. We have learned from quantum physics that we have the choice of how we wish to shape time. We have many opportunities to practice changing fear into peace. Whenever we hear or see actions or words that are not peace-filled, let's change them in our minds to peaceful thoughts. Sometimes they may be thoughts inside ourselves that we have to catch and reel in like a fish back to our positive center. We are both the fishermen and the fish.

Each time we send out the Light of our peace-filled thoughts, we are changing the world, one person at a time. Change of consciousness occurs one by one until finally, enough people have made the change.

Many people have begun the daily practice of sending out the Light of peace to people everywhere until the whole world is filled with peace. When I look at this photo, I can sense, in the sky, the spreading of the Light of Peace.

Here's to joining together and increasing the Inner Peace of all.

MAY - Inner Blossoms

This flower is part of a magnificent magnolia tree where I used to live. Every May it sends out its amazing blossoms before it sends out its leaves, as you can see in this picture. I had never heard of a tree making its flowers before its leaves. This tree became my May landmark, reminding me to think of our inner blossoms and not to always wait for our leaves to arrive.   The flowers we give to life are what we contribute to make this a better world. Each of us has unique gifts that we have come to Earth to share. At exactly the perfect moment in our lives, we will use them to help and inspire others. Since we are always growing, we flower over and over again at many different times in our lives.

Think about your gifts and how you use them to create more beauty, more joy, and more love in the world. How do you contribute beauty? Are you a gardener, a quilter, a photographer, an artist? Do you learn about herbs and crystals to help others with their healing? Do you offer unique ideas or share stories of how you have overcome obstacles to find greater happiness? Do you smile at people when you pass them to brighten their day? We each have both tangible and intangible gifts to give. Each time we help someone by listening and helping them feel appreciated and loved, we have given our intangible gifts.

To rephrase an old saying, "As we give, so shall we receive." The more aware we are of all our blessings, the more peace-filled we become. May is a month to think about the abundance in our lives. If you start to think of what you don't have, catch the thought and change it to what you do have. If it's a cloudy day, notice how much brighter the colors in Nature are on such days.

I begin every morning by looking out my window to an inspiring view of a mountain range and an ever-changing sky. As I breathe in, I thank God, all my Guides and Angels, and all my loved ones on Earth and in Heaven for their blessings. Then I add, "Please keep up the good work!", which I hope makes them smile.

Our ongoing practice in deeply receiving the beauty and abundance in our lives is a major key to increasing our Inner Peace. Just to fully breathe in fresh air is a wonderful cause for gratitude.

What are you grateful for in your life? Do you see the eternal circle of giving and receiving? Inner Peace asks us to be aware of both.

Happy Gratefulness Month!

JUNE - Water Your Self

Can you hear the school bell ringing? "School's out", it's singing, "Let the summer begin!" Can you remember what it felt like as a child on that last day of school? Were you excited about the coming months? Did you go to the beach or to camp? Did you have to work? Did you spend time lying on the lawn, looking up at the passing clouds? What they called "doing nothing" at all was actually a practice in living in the present moment. It was our meditation, our reconnection with Nature.

And now? How will you greet this upcoming time? Will you fill all the spaces with activity? Will you work as much? Will you connect with Nature's slower pace? It's trying hard to tell us to slow down and listen. If you have a garden, pay close attention to how each plant is growing. They grow very slowly, perhaps encouraging us to find a proper pace.

Plants need sunlight. The Sun is a symbol for the Divine. Plants remind us to place ourselves where we can receive divine messages. Some plants need strong sunlight; some need sun and shade. How do you grow? How much independence do you need to grow? Do you need to read? to rest? to listen to music? to have time to do nothing? What nurtures you in the summer? Do you breathe in deeply the fragrance of the earth? There is a replenishing vibration in the soil helping us to become more grounded and connected with true growth. Do you talk to your plants? They can hear you. Do you talk to your Highest Self? It hears you too.

Set your Intention at the beginning and ending of each day for exactly what you would like to achieve for that day. Would you like to enjoy the day more? Would you like to feel more relaxed and at peace? Tell your Self what you would like by Setting your Intention. Your thoughts will become your reality. That is how we water our Selves and open to the Sun.

Happy Intending!

JULY - Peaceful Patterns

Imagine you are entering the world of my photo. This Japanese garden in Toulouse, France captures for me the essence of life's peaceful movement. The master gardeners have designed it with a goal of peace so we don't feel disturbed by its motion. Each series of lines is different and yet each group fits together.

Life also has an Order, although we may not always be aware of it. All that happens is part of a larger plan created by the Good to teach us that Life is a good learning process. Of course, we all experience difficult times. When we are experiencing them, we may not think of them as necessary, but once we have an overview and understand the reasons for it all, an amazing sense of Order and Peace emerges. Like the garden, seeing the whole brings us a deep sense of calm.

In your own home or garden, look for the peaceful patterns you have created with furniture, art or plants. Try to feel a sense of the whole in your own peace-filled patterns. The more we can see the serenity behind life's movement, the greater our inner sense of peace will be.

To help our inner garden grow, we must water the seeds of our Patience and Understanding. If we could observe our lives through the eyes of the Divine, we would know the truth of "all things in their time". We would understand the positive reasons for all the lessons. That understanding is the foundation of acceptance and a major key to Inner Peace. Since we can't have all the answers right now, we must grow our inner gardens with Faith, the belief that there is a Positive Purpose and Order in all of Life. We often say, "Seeing is believing". Faith is believing before we see the results. The deeper our Faith, the stronger our Inner Peace.

May you water your seeds of Faith
with Hope and Love.

AUGUST –
The Gift of Who We Are

In this third month of summer, the Sun is my theme. It is what we look for every day. When we arise, the first thing we look for is what kind of day it will be, i.e. how brightly the Sun will shine.

My photo this month is one of the great gifts of the Sun, a rainbow. We are all fascinated by this dazzling display of colors after a rainstorm. And we all wonder what and where is the Pot of Gold it promises. As I wrote in my DVD *Messages from Nature*, "The Pot of Gold is a symbol of what we learn from the storms of our difficulties." No matter what the challenge, there is always a gift in the lesson it brings. Our job is to search for the positive lesson. When we listen to the news and all the horrendous events, we have to look at the positive responses from individuals and communities for our hope. Each difficulty we encounter is a positive lesson and an opportunity to grow, and therefore, a gift.

What is the gift of each day? The Sun is our first and last gift since it begins and ends each day. It symbolizes the Light of understanding and therefore the Light of the Divine in each of us. The Sun asks us to know and give our gifts throughout our lives. That is why we are here on Earth. Ask yourself, What are your gifts and how do you give them? Are there gifts you would like to increase or develop? How might you do that?

Another dimension of giving and receiving is gratitude ... recognizing the gifts we are given every day and acknowledging them. It is a good idea to create a daily gratitude list. Once you begin to write down what you are grateful for each day, you will see how many blessings you've been given. There are blessings of people, of Nature, and of Love. And then there is one blessing that we may tend to forget ... the gift of our lessons that help us to grow. The harder the lesson, the greater the opportunity for growth.

Being aware of our blessings helps to increase our Inner Peace by leaps and bounds every day. It makes us more present to the moment where all happiness exists. No matter what we call it, mindfulness or living in the Present, that is where we can best see and feel life's gifts.

Since the Sun is a symbol of the Divine, we are also being asked to recognize the Divine Self in every person. No matter where we are in our evolution, we are each a piece of the Divine. The Self within us is always filled with the peace of this knowledge. When you wish someone *Namaste*, which means *I salute the Divine in You*, remember that we are each a piece of that great gift.

Seek your Self and the Self in others and you will understand the meaning of *Namaste* more deeply every day.

I salute the Divine in You!

SEPTEMBER - Seeing the Good

    Every fall I am moved by the beauty that Nature shows us. At the perfect moment each leaf suddenly bursts with color. One flaming tree can light up an entire road. So it is with people - one positive thought inspires us all.

    The wonderful autumnal path in this photo reminds us that we are keeping one eye on the present and one eye on the future, wondering what it will bring. None of us knows what lies ahead, but we can remain positive, knowing there is a reason for everything.

    We cannot change what happens, but we do have control over our reactions. Every time we believe in and search for a positive outcome, we add to the Light that will help everyone and everything on our beautiful planet. Let's set our minds and hearts on seeing the Good in all things even when times are challenging.

*Positive Belief will increase the Peace
in everyone around us.*

OCTOBER - Your Beauty

It is the time of Ooooohs and Aaaaahs as October makes its presence known. Look over there …. and there …. and there. Each flaming tree is more spectacular than the last. Despite what kind of summer we've had and how much rainfall we did or didn't receive, the trees infallibly put on their best colors to amaze us.

Scientists have proven that inside each leaf, the colors it will become are already stored. As the daylight hours decrease and the tree makes less and less chlorophyll, the pigments that were already present in the leaf begin to show their brilliant oranges, yellows and reds. What does this mean philosophically? It tells us that, like the colors stored in leaves, we came to Earth with our gifts stored inside us as potential. But each of us must wait until the Perfect Time for those gifts to emerge so we can show our true colors. That's why we can bloom and bloom again at any age. After all, life is for continual growth toward greater understanding and love.

Look again at those spectacular fall trees. They are you. October's colors remind us of our own beauty. Here are some exercises to do in this glorious month.

- Look in the mirror of your Soul. Look past imperfections to see your full inner beauty. The more you look, the more you will see.

- Look around you at all the people in your life to see their beauty. Let them know what you see.

- Be especially aware of how each color you see on an autumn tree "in bloom" affects you. The more sensitive you are to your own reactions, the clearer your perception will be.

- If you don't already do this, practice feeling gratitude for all the beauty that you are and see.

October presents us with a special opportunity. The more we see our own inner beauty, the more it inspires peace in everyone around you. So, go ahead and be your most Beautiful Self.

Always see the Beauty in your Life!

NOVEMBER –
Gratefulness is Peace

November, the month of transition, has arrived, reminding us the year is heading for its end. As we look up, we see the signs of change in everything from the skies to the golden pine needles in this photo. Change is the only thing that remains constant in life.

To grow, we must change. What strikes me most about the beautiful pine needles in the photo is the glorious autumn light streaming through them. As daylight decreases each day, we have to focus on whatever light we can see. That reminds us to feel and remember the light in our hearts that is always there. On a day when there is less sunshine, we must be the sunshine.

There is a kind of nostalgia that permeates this month as we look back and ahead. It reminds us that life is an endless cycle. Symbolically, it asks us to let go of all that has ended and trust that each new, unknown moment will be better.

Nature is our great teacher, reminding us that we have to let go of what has ended to make room for next year's growth. Our test is to remember that every ending is also a new beginning, that Life will always bring us to a better place, in spite of what is showing in the present moment.

November represents the intangible truth of Life, all that cannot be seen or touched but goes on forever. Because of this, it reminds us of our loved ones that we can no longer see and touch, all the people and animals who have left this Earth. They want us to know there is no death and are sending us love from the peaceful place where they are now, hoping that we will feel their love.

In November, when there are fewer blooming flowers for us to admire, we appreciate any color that is showing. This season of harvest fills us with a desire to share our blessings with those whose harvest is smaller. As we focus on the Light we have, we are filled with gratitude for our blessings. Gratefulness is a major part of Inner Peace. The gift of November, like the gift of life itself, is one that keeps on giving and giving.

May we see our Blessings.

DECEMBER - An Age of Change

I chose this photo for December for many reasons. When we think of this month, we think of a star leading the Wise Men, who were astrologers, to the Divine Baby. We think of Christmas lights at night and all the beautiful decorations people place in and on their homes. In addition, we are faced with the darkness in the world, such as the violent events we have seen in so many places.

It is an especially challenging time to maintain a balance between righteous indignation, sadness and upset, and an equally strong desire to create inner and outer peace. We have no control over the violent events that happen but we do have control over our reactions. We may find ourselves asking, Why is this happening? What is the best way to react? These are most important, complex questions.

We have read and heard about groups violently protesting, about people who are trying to exert power over others and frighten them into submission. These are all signs of the difficult times we live in. Why are they happening? Behind these events there is a larger answer.

We are now in the Age of Aquarius which is approximately from the year 2,000-4,000. Aquarius is the astrological sign and symbol for Major Change. You can witness its effects, not only in people's reactions but also in climate changes, volcanic eruptions, and earthquakes. Some of them are caused by the misuse of our resources but some are a part of the Major Change. We are being asked to stretch and reach out to all people everywhere. We are being asked to become One World where we will all work together for the betterment of all humankind, all creatures, and the Earth itself. These are some of the themes of Aquarius.

Resistance and fear are the ego reaction of many people to change. These reactions often lead to violence and certainly to difficulties. How can we best react to all that is happening?

- By understanding this is all about the need for positive change
- By accepting that life is change
- By reacting with compassion, love, and faith in positive outcomes

We must understand how frightened people are of change. It is only when we maintain the faith to know that all change is and will be positive that we can embrace it with an open heart and mind.

In this holiday season, it would be wonderful to emulate the Wise Men and seek out the Light of positive change. In the darkest of times, it is the Light that leads us to truth and peace. Stay in touch with your own inner Light as you observe the changes in the world and understand the fear that creates negative reactions. Balance these difficulties by seeking the wonder and beauty in each day. Focus on all that you love. These are all part of the Truth of life. Let us stand together in our ongoing search for Inner Peace until, like the ocean, the ripples of our search reach out to the whole world.

With that thought,

I wish you all
Loving Seasons of Peace.

BeCause and Effect

JANUARY - Acceptance

If you enter my photo in your imagination, we are standing at the water's edge on the crisp white snow. The air is winter cool. Take a deep breath and breathe in its purity. It is sunrise and the sun's glorious pink reflections are singing to us on the distant horizon. We are up early to greet this new day and can see its potential. We are witnessing together the sacred possibilities that begin each new day.

If you look closely at the left side of the photo, you will see a man-made light reflection. It's a perfect symbol of the message that we must carry our own inner light and also be nourished by nature's light.

The same is true for the New Year. The doors of hope and peace are both inside us and in front of us. Nature holds within it all of life's messages and truths. The truth of each new day is that peace is there for the receiving.

January, the first month of a new year, is also the symbol of morning as we begin again. The seasons and months exist to remind us that life and growth are part of an eternal cycle. The cycle of growth is a spiral so that as we return to the same month on the spiral, we are in a new place on the spiral that reflects how much we've learned and grown. "What about all the people who haven't changed and grown?", I hear you asking? They, too, are learning, even if only in the unconscious. We may not see other people's changes but they are still working on their chosen lessons. All our tests continue even if we think we're ignoring them. Learning, like life, is eternal.

There are many tests in Life. The greatest of these is the test of faith that every person will find peace at the Perfect Time. Our individual job is to believe that Truth, and to continue deepening our inner peace, no matter what is happening around us and in the world.

Inner peace is our birthright if we choose to accept it. We cannot give it to anyone else, but we can fully receive and appreciate its ongoing blessing and live in its joy. We can be a shining example of a commitment to live in Inner Peace.

Inner Peace is acceptance. Once we know that everything is a lesson to help us grow, then we can accept where everyone is on the continuum of learning. We can know and trust there is a larger plan for Good and that we are each watched over and guided every step of the way.

May we each increase our Inner Peace every New Year!

FEBRUARY - Symbols of Hope

    February is a time for us to gain the wisdom of perspective. Whenever we feel stressed or overwhelmed, we can slow down our minds and mentally move ourselves to a greater distance. Then we can calmly look for the messages and information that are there for us. Thinking of that concept, notice the covered bridge in my photo, far up ahead. It is bathed in sunlight. Life is often best understood when we search for the symbolic meaning in our messages and dreams. In the photo, the covered bridge seems like a symbol of the time to come.

    Bridges are often the symbol of transitions, our inner movement to a newer place. When you think of your own future, try to imagine the covered bridges in your life. They represent something that protects us from the "elements" while allowing us to move forward comfortably. In a time of major change, we all need that protection to ease our way.

Look far down the river to the bridge and visualize what you would like in the upcoming time. Clearly stating what we want is the first step to making it a reality. It is the key to manifestation. What would you like to add into your life? Now, practice making your wishes flexible just in case life finds a better way than what you've planned. Just as we plant seeds in our spring garden, we plant mental seeds in our February garden.

Now that you've clarified your own wishes, try expanding your image to seeing a happier, healthier, more peace-filled world. Don't worry about how it will happen. Just envision it existing. That is an important part of planting the seed, something we can each do. If we each add our own image to our collective desire for Inner Peace, we will move its reality closer.

In my vision, I see all the people of the world living at peace with one another, having plenty to eat, doing fulfilling work they enjoy and having proper clothing and shelter to help them enjoy each season on this beautiful Earth. Now is the time for you to create your own vision.

Happy Imagining!

MARCH - Patience Creates Peace

Doesn't my photo just say it all! Here we are in March and our minds are saying, "Where's the picnic with all this snow? We've got the tables out! Why is it taking so long???"

There is so much we want to do in our lives and for this world and it seems like it's taking so long to happen. What's the lesson? It's about Patience.

The more patience we have, the deeper our Inner Peace. So the question is, what gives us patience?

The simple answer is Faith

- that there is a Divine Plan for us all.
- that Life is always moving in a more peaceful direction.
- that others will become kinder and more peace-filled in time.

- that all we hope for in this world will come to be.
- that we are all here to learn the lessons we've chosen.

- that we will all learn our lessons in our own unique timing.

I can hear some of you saying, "In time". But how long will it take? Since life has only Perfect Timing, it will happen at exactly the right time.

One question that comes up is "What can I do to move it along in a positive direction?"

The answer is: Trust in Life's goodness. Have the faith to know that everything that happens is a lesson. Once we've learned it, that lesson ends. One ongoing lesson we all have is to keep choosing a peace-filled optimistic response from moment to moment. Our awareness of that ongoing choice helps us to live in the Present, which is where all happiness exists.

We live in complex times. The simple response to the complex is to believe in positive outcomes and to choose a peaceful response to every situation. Truth is both simple and complex. The simple side asks us to shine the Light of Optimism at all times.

Here's to our mutual support of one another's patience and Inner Peace.

APRIL - Delightful Reactions

What was your first reaction to my April photo? Did you laugh? Did you say, "Uh oh"? Did you feel a sense of disappointment?

My photo this month was not meant as a forecast but rather to give us an opportunity to observe our reactions. Maintaining a sense of Inner Peace means we have to find a delightful and positive way to react to whatever comes our way. We all have expectations and our thoughts of April are no exception. What makes each moment so special is that we are always given a chance to find something to feel grateful for, no matter what we were hoping for.

Recently I had a dream that told me to carry rubber bands with me wherever I go and to share that thought with all my friends. As soon as I awoke, my first reaction was to put a bunch of rubber bands in a Ziploc bag and carry them to my car. Then I came inside and laughed, realizing that my dream was a symbolic message about being flexible and stretching.

That's why I chose this fun April photo. The charming table and chairs are awaiting picnics but life may have other plans. The picnics will come but now it is time to choose our most delightful reactions. It's easy to say, "Don't have expectations; just live in the Present", but being human, we will have hopes for different situations. What matters most are our moment-to-moment reactions to whatever life brings. Rather than being disappointed, we can laugh and find something positive. Every time we do, we have deepened our commitment to Inner Peace.

I wish you all zany fun-filled months!!!

MAY - Feel the Hope

Everyone has anxiously awaited the month of May and at last, as promised, it has arrived. May, the first month of spring, is the herald of this new season. When we look at the many shades of greens in my picture, we can feel the hope it offers. Green is the color of peace and growth. Let yourself feel in your mind the first warm breezes of spring. They are soft like many of the greens you see here.

When I listen to people's conversation each day, I hear how often we forget the gifts of each season. On a cloudy day, people feel down and don't seem to remember that the sun is just behind the clouds. In spring, nature reminds us firsthand that the sun has always been there, waiting patiently behind the winter.

Every day, **WE** must be the sunshine to everyone and everything in our lives. That knowledge is part of our daily practice on Inner Peace if we accept the challenge. Whether the sun is shining or not, we must remember it is always there.

When we are feeling impatient with what's happening in our lives and in the world, it is helpful to look to spring and its message of peace and abundance. Look at my photo again and think of the bridge as a symbol of a new beginning, a walkway into a future we must create.

Let's look far down the road and plant seeds of hope now. Picture how you would like the world to be. I would like to see a planet of peace and harmony where people help one another, where we all take good care of the Earth, a place where we appreciate our blessings. If each of us concentrates on a peaceful image, we will plant the seeds of peace in our world. Just as we can't see any growth springing up after we've planted the first seeds, we must still water them every day and wait patiently for them to grow. In the same way, we must water our image of Peace every day by sending out our image of Light and hope for the future. Then, in time, it will happen.

I join each of you in a celebration
of new Growth and new Peace.

JUNE

Clear Sight

My June photos were taken at the Botanical Gardens in Montreal. Look closely at the colors and you will notice that some colors are faded and some are clear. Part of each photo is an illusion. Can you tell which part is which?

If you look closely, the background of the first photo is faded and the top right background in the second photo is wrinkled, with part of it not showing. Why? Because those parts are a painting, not a photo. What is real in the photos? Only the birds in the water and the stones near them and directly behind them are real. When I first saw the scene, I did not realize that part of the scene was an illusion.

Why have I chosen these photos? They are a metaphor for life, asking us to see what is real and what is only in our own minds. How often do we add in our own thoughts and feelings as we look at life and not see what is real? To truly "see", we must look with a non-judgmental, understanding eye. Since we cannot ever know the whole picture, we must accept that there is a reason for everything. If we are not understanding certain people or situations, that is a lesson for us. As my photos illustrate often the whole truth is not apparent.

Our job, in all situations, is to hold onto the Light of Truth, to know that there is a Positive Source behind all of Life and that in time we will learn and become more understanding. As we see the larger picture, the more we will learn that whatever is happening is a lesson to make us stronger, kinder and more loving. We are here on earth to help and care for one another so that, in time, there will be peace. Peace begins one heart at a time. As each of us increases our faith in Life's positive nature and purpose, no matter how difficult the outside picture, the more we will help the world move toward the ultimate goal of a peaceful world of caring people.

    Inner peace comes when we redefine all things as Positive. It begins with knowing that whatever the symbolic or actual "weather", whether it's raining, snowing, stormy, cloudy or sunny, it's all good. There is no such thing as a bad day unless we decide it is. That is always our choice. There is so much we cannot know but we can believe that in time, it will all be good as we evolve. This is an ongoing practice for each of us.

Happy Practicing!

JULY - Finding Home

After an unusually cool spring and cold but dry winter, many people have wondered if summer is really going to stay. This brings us to the question of security and what we can trust. Deep within each of us, there is a great need to feel secure and reassured.

What makes you feel secure? Is it living in a certain town? Is it knowing that you feel safe to hike, walk or swim? Is it knowing you are surrounded by family and friends who love you? Is it knowing you have and will have enough money to pay bills and live in your home?

Then there is the question: What is home? Is it a place? a person? people? pets? Is it being with one person or with people and animals who love and accept you? Is it being surrounded by familiar objects that remind you of special times and people?

Often, as we age and no longer want the responsibilities of owning a house, some of us sell our homes to be closer to family. Some move to a senior residence, or move in with a family member. As we prepare to move, we enter a time of paring down, which is a redefining of what things we need to feel at home. None of us can be sure that we will always live where we are right now. So, the question of home becomes a larger consideration. How can we find a sense of home, no matter where we live? Since change is inevitable, we must work to see its positive nature. The picture I chose for July seems to me a symbol for the waters of Time.

How can we always feel that we are home? For me, it is an ongoing search to find a sense of home inside myself, no matter where I am. I will be traveling to France this summer and staying at many different places. If I feel at home in myself, I will feel secure no matter where I go. If I carry the home that is Me within me, I will always be home. My journey seems to mirror the changing nature of life itself.

The song "Going Home" from Dvorak's New World symphony often makes me think of the place I think we came from and will return to when we leave this Earth. I see Heaven as a place where the air and water and light are pure and clean and beautiful and where we are loved unconditionally. I believe that we came here to recreate those conditions on Earth. If we look around us, we know we have a great deal of work to do, but we know our goal.

One by one, as we re-create Heaven's Peace, we will create Peace both within and without.

AUGUST - The Gift of Balance

August has arrived and has brought with it, the fullness of summer, as you can see in these beautiful flowers from my current garden.

I recently read that imagination is the highest level of Spirituality, perhaps because it puts us in touch with the Peaceful Kingdom where we all came from and where we will return some day. This month I am going to ask you to indulge in some thoughts of imagination.

This summer, for the first time, I can actually feel the smiles in my own flower garden. I never knew my flowers smiled before. If you look carefully at the flower below, you can almost feel it speaking. I sense that they are all teaching us about peace through their example.

Flowers don't have to do anything to be peace-filled, as they enjoy the sun shining on them and take in the soothing breezes. Even in a storm, they are peace-filled since they accept all that comes. They don't ask anything of us but to water, feed and appreciate them. What a lovely definition of Love.

When I think of our lives and apply it to the flowers, they provide a yardstick for us. All our lives are busy by necessity. Birds and flowers and Nature remind us there is more to Life than only working. Nature reminds us that we need to make some time every day to just enjoy life. Have we forgotten to balance our work with rest? Part of every day needs to be a mini vacation or some time away from our work. When we stop and rest and take in nature's replenishment, we can create balance, a major ingredient of Inner Peace.

I hear the essence of nature's teachings in this quote from *The Peaceful Climb* by the late Yvonne Youst, "You must come to know the value of rest. Breathe out with work and activity to give to Life. Breathe in with rest and stillness to be replenished by Life. You are a human tree on the Earth. Do not pursue distraction because you fear that rest is a kind of death. You must learn to rest to truly feel the value of being alive."

I am eternally grateful to our teachers in Nature for their lessons in Peace.

SEPTEMBER- Becoming Better

What a wonderful reminder we see in this photo. Life asks us to look at all the little places in our life that are growing and filled with beauty. So often we walk right past them and never notice. As summer comes to an end and a new season begins, a new cycle opens up. It is the cycle of learning and improving. Small wonder that school begins each fall. We are each "going back" to learn something new.

All of us are here on Earth to learn our lessons and help one another with our gifts. September is the part of the cycle that reminds us of that and asks us to study something we value. Every time we learn something new, we inevitably make mistakes. But the true test is how we deal with the error. Do we get down on ourselves and become depressed and upset? Do we obsess about the mistake? Shakespeare once said "To err is human." To balance that, we must add: Now stand back up when you've fallen off your symbolic bicycle, brush yourself off, and go forward with more understanding. That's the key. What is that mistake trying to teach us? What is the lesson we're asking ourselves to learn? As we answer these questions, we must remind ourselves to look without judgment so that we can understand and correct our course. We do have the right to evaluate what is not right. What we must not do is judge the error.

What is the difference between Judgment and Evaluation? It is objectivity. We have to look at our mistakes with an impartial, non-emotional eye. If we are thankful for the lesson, rather than being upset and chiding ourselves, we can learn happily and get right back on the bicycle of forward motion.

The September questions I would ask you to consider are:

✶What lesson or lessons are you working on?   ✶How are you doing? Are you moving forward patiently, being kind to yourself and grateful for your lesson? ✶What is the next step you will want to take because of this lesson?

To be alive is to grow, expand and change. Think of the beautiful pine in the photo. Let it remind you to appreciate your ongoing growth and the growth of everyone and everything in your life.

Remember that we are wonderful today and will be even better tomorrow. Repeating this sentence helps us accept the Present and have the humility to know we are always growing and improving. It's a major key to Inner Peace.

Enjoy becoming better!

October –
Awareness Creates Peace

Every October greets us with its unique combinations of color. Each year I look forward to the magnificent displays in my favorite places and to the fun of searching for new wonderful scenes to enjoy.

If we think of the four seasons as a huge 360 °circle, autumn sits 180° away from spring, its opposite side and complement. If spring teaches us how to move forward with the excitement of youth, autumn shows us how to look at life with the reflection and wisdom of age.

No matter what our age, it asks us to consider what we have learned from the time just past. Nature is our constant teacher, even when we aren't aware of its lessons. In fall we notice that outer growth in Nature is slowing down. The ancient peoples lived by the cycles of Nature, but in our overly busy lives, we rarely make time to notice what changes have taken place. What was different or new? Perhaps it's our reactions that have changed.

    Nature reminds us that each of us is always changing and growing, even when we aren't conscious of how we've changed.   The more we become aware of our growth, the more our Inner Peace and joy will expand. Autumn reassures us that every new period can be glorious. Imagine the difference in how you'd feel if you quickly passed by a magnificent flower bed without even looking at it or if you slowed down to notice the special beauty of each flower and took the time to admire the whole garden. Every time we stop, look, and take in Fall's splendor, we increase our joy and our Inner Peace.

    As we admire the glory of this autumn, I hope we will each, in our own unique ways, nurture the Nature that has nurtured us.

Happy Glorious Life to all of you!!

NOVEMBER - Deepening Our Peace

What a complex world we live in and how complicated the times seem to be. That is the exact moment to search for the other side of the coin, the simple truth.

The first of the simple truths is: We all have two parts within us, Ego and Self. I am not using the word Ego here as it is often used.

- The **Ego** is fear and manifests itself as either anger or sadness. It always blames the other and will do anything to be sure it is always right. It is impatient and wants what it wants immediately. It is either too focused on what it wants or too worried about what others think.

- The **Self** is the part in each of us that is a part of the Divine. It is always reaching up to learn more, always seeking joy, more gratitude and finding the wonder in every day. It knows we are all here to learn whatever lessons we have chosen and that as we learn them, we will become more fulfilled, more joy-filled. The Self knows that life is meant for us to be happy, to help and love one another. It knows that everything will be better in time. Simply put, the Self is our faith in the goodness of life.

We are in challenging times. We can observe unrest and anger everywhere. What is the job of the Self in such times? It is to become even more understanding, to send out our Light to all people, to ask for and hope for peace everywhere. Peace begins inside every one of us. We must consistently choose a peace-filled reaction in every circumstance. The choice is always there. If we want peace, we must be it.

As you look at my November photo, see yourself choosing to see the Light-filled colors and the beauty in this late autumn scene. Feel the freshness in the air asking us to appreciate every aspect in every season. Every day has a gift when we open our eyes and See.

There is a positive reason behind all things. In changing times, we must constantly search for optimism, the Positive behind all that happens. We must deepen our Inner Peace so we can spread it to everyone. This is the message in the embers of November.

Happy Spreading the Seeds of Peace!!!

DECEMBER -
White, Light, and Snow

As we begin this last month of the year, I can hear the din of voices everywhere frantically making lists of all that needs to be done before the year is over. It is a cacophony of stressful sound... not one we wish to hear!

That's why I chose this photo. Whether we are blessed with lots of snow or not in December, the snow is one magical reminder of the Peace of Earth. In its silence, it wraps the Earth in peace. As you look at the photo, you can feel the snow asking us to join its peaceful vibration. It reminds us to make some time every day for breathing in that Peace. With all the difficulty in the world and perhaps in your life, we need that calm every day.

If you begin to feel the potential overload, stop yourself, breathe in slowly and as you breathe out, choose Inner Peace. It is a moment-to-moment choice we make. And we receive many opportunities to practice that choice! I find it helpful to hold on to the image in this photo at challenging moments. It returns me to the choice I have made, to make every day a joyful, positive day. Even if we falter at times, we can continue to practice choosing the restful comfort of Peace.

The more Inner Peace you feel, the easier it is to be understanding and patient of others' challenges. Then we can accept where they are on their journey and love them as they are.

All the great spiritual paths are devoted to helping us reach for and maintain peace, compassion and love for all people, whether through meditation, prayer or sending out positive thoughts.

As we experience the month of the shortest amount of sunlight and watch the cycle slowly increase to greater light, we remember that darkness, a symbol for difficulties, causes a yearning in every person for Light. We appreciate the Light even more when there are less hours of daylight and find ourselves deepening our appreciation of our blessings.

Thank you for allowing me to share my thoughts of Peace with you.

EPILOGUE

My exploration of the ways we can achieve greater Inner Peace has been and continues to be a wonderful journey. If I were to give an overview, I would say that Inner Peace comes from knowing that Life is a series of ongoing lessons and that there is something Positive to be found in every lesson and every day. This is a belief and practice I live. I also have come to deeply accept that there is only Perfect Timing which has helped me become very patient. One key to Inner Peace is accepting all people no matter where they are in their journey. Once we know we are all a work in progress, we can feel compassion for the mad/sad Ego and love the Divine Self in every person.

Yvonne Youst explains it clearly in *The Peaceful Climb* when she says, "There is a Peaceful Kingdom. It exists through all eternity. This Kingdom is around you in all rooms. It surrounds you when you go outside, beneath the circling sky. Peace is always near you but it cannot cross the threshold until you open your door. The handle of that door is Love."

I hope my thoughts and photos will be a help to you as you explore your own Inner Peace. They are written from my heart in my own ongoing search to increase my Inner Peace. Our peace-filled thoughts and love reach out to touch everyone in our lives. World peace occurs one peaceful person at a time.

ABOUT THE AUTHOR

Susan Ackerman lives in Northern New Hampshire. She has Master's Degrees in Teaching and Counseling. As a spiritual teacher, astrologer and counselor for 36 years, she has given many courses and workshops in New England on Inner Peace, Stress Reduction and Messages from Nature. She is the author of *Beginnings and Endings*, *The Gift of Time*, *Comforting Thoughts, The Spiritual Collection* and *Ella's Journey from Sadness to Hope*. She is co-author, with Yvonne Youst, of *Christmas is in the Air, All About New Hampshire,* and *New Hampshuh Tales.*

To contact her, write to sackerman@lifeinsightastrology.com or visit her website: lifeinsightastrology.com

www.ingramcontent.com/pod-product-compliance
Lightning Source LLC
Chambersburg PA
CBHW050815090426
42736CB00021B/3463